Fun with GRAMMAR

Book 2

Published in Moonstone
by Rupa Publications India Pvt. Ltd 2023
7/16, Ansari Road, Daryaganj
New Delhi 110002

Sales centres:
Prayagraj Bengaluru Chennai
Hyderabad Jaipur Kathmandu
Kolkata Mumbai

P-ISBN: 978-93-5702-343-6
E-ISBN: 978-93-5702-327-6

First impression 2023

10 9 8 7 6 5 4 3 2 1

Printed in India

CONTENTS

NOUNS

Nouns *are words that name people, places, animals, things, or ideas.*

Example:

Abraham Lincoln, Shahrukh Khan (person)

London, Delhi (place)

Dog, Elephant (animals)

Table, Chair (things)

Justice, Honesty (idea)

Types of Nouns

Nouns are of four types as follows –

- **Common noun**
- **Proper noun**
- **Collective noun**
- **Abstract noun**

Let us discuss them one by one -

Common Noun

A common noun is used to refer to the general or generic name of person, place, animal and things.

Example:

- I am reading a **book**.
- My **mother** is cooking **food**.

Proper Noun

A proper noun is used to refer to a specific person, place or object.

Example:

- **Paris** is the capital of **France.**
- **Jawaharlal Nehru** was the first prime minister of **India.**

A Is the highlighted word in the sentence a common noun or a proper noun?

1. My friend grew up in a small town. ______________
2. Let me introduce you to Mary. ______________
3. He is the chairman of the British Broadcasting Corporation. ______________
4. The books are on your desk ______________, ______________
5. I have two dogs. ______________
6. Karen played with her sister. ______________, ______________
7. Fran went to Furry Friends Pet Shop. ______________, ______________
8. The teacher punished the mischievous boy. ______________, ______________

B Underline the common noun and circle the proper noun in each sentence.

1. Rita went to the market to buy vegetables.
2. Ayush left his cricket kit at my house.
3. My brother is a well-known dentist.
4. My aunt is a nice lady.
5. Mr. Stilton is a good writer.
6. Akbar was a great emperor.
7. This road is very narrow.

COLLECTIVE NOUNS

A* collective noun *denotes a group of people or animals or things.

Examples: class (group of students), pride (group of lions), crew (group of sailors)

The **fleet** of ships has reached the coast.

The **gang** of dacoits has been caught.

Collective nouns can be treated as singular or plural.

A Complete the following sentences with a collective noun given in the box below:

choir	fleet	crowd	pack
library	swarm	bouquet	shoal

1. There was a roar from the ________ of spectators when the home team won.

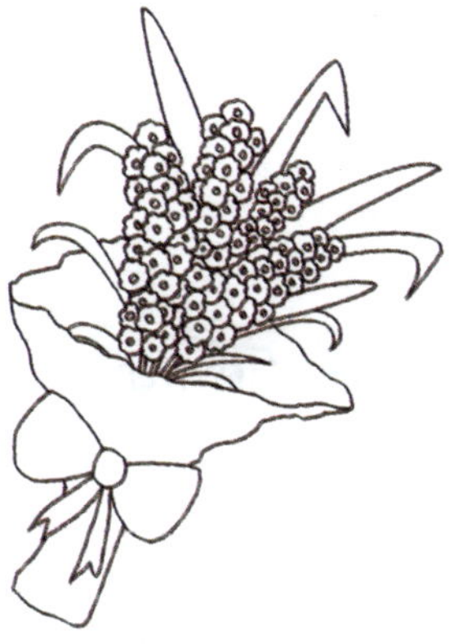

2. Nancy gave her mother a ________ of flowers on her birthday.

3. A ________ of singers is performing on the stage.

4. A ________ of ships arrived at the dock.

5. The ________ of wolves roamed through the forest.

6. Peter has his own ________ of books.

7. We saw a ________ of fish swimming alongside the river bank.

8. A ________ of bees flew out of the bush.

B Match the suitable collective noun with each group.

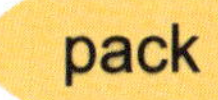

flock

army

team

herd

loaf

PRONOUNS

***A pronoun** is a word that takes the place of a noun in a sentence.* **Pronouns** *are used to avoid repeating the same nouns over and over again.*

For **Example**, "Jeremy ran so fast, you'd think his life was on the line."

Types of Pronouns

Pronouns can be divided into several categories:

personal, possessive, relative, demonstrative, interrogative, and reflexive.

Personal pronouns

Personal pronouns are always *specific* and are often used to *replace a proper noun* (someone's name) or a *collective group of people or things.*

There are two types of personal pronouns: subject and object.

When the person or thing is the subject of the sentence,* subject pronouns *are used, such as I, you, he, she, it, we, they.

Examples:

- I like to watch TV, but he does not.
- She struck him on the nose.

He did not study hard for the exam.

Object pronouns *are used when the person or thing is the object of the sentence, such as me, you, him, her, it, us, you, them.*

Examples:

- Sonia likes me but hates him.
- Missing the bus will make us late.
- Don't tell her the truth.

We will be late if **you** don't hurry up.

In the above sentence, ***we*** *is the subject of the sentence, but* ***you*** *is the object.*

A **Use these pronouns to complete Peter's description of his family. You may use some pronouns more than once.**

he	it	I	she	we	they	us

Hello, my name is Peter. ______ live in the city with my mother and father and two sisters. My father is a teacher. ______ works very long hours. My mother is a lawyer, but ______ only works part - time. My sisters and I try to help our parents as much as ______ can. My sisters help in the kitchen. ______ wash and dry the dishes. ______ make my own bed and keep my room tidy. ______ have a cat called Ginger. ______ has lived with ______ for a long time.

B **Write the nouns that are referred to by the pronouns in bold print in the sentence in the space provided. The first one is done for you.**

1. The Eiffel Tower is a famous building. **It** took two years to build.

   Eiffel Tower

2. Dad and I cycled to the seaside. **We** went there to fish.

   ____

3. Meet Andrew and Tom. **They** are brothers.

____

4. Hi, Sonia! How are **you**?

____

5. The wind was so strong, **it** uprooted some trees.

____

6. John, Sue and I often go to the playground. **We** play basketball there.

____

7. This computer is too slow. We must replace **it**.

____

8. Your shoes are dirty. Go and wash **them**.

____

9. Do you remember Alice? **She** is my cousin.

____

10. Last Sunday, Kathy married a nice young man called Tim. **He** is the manager of a bookshop.

____

Possessive Pronouns

Possessive pronouns ***show ownership or possession of a noun such as my, our, your, his, her, its (note there is no apostrophe), their.***

Example:

- Is that **my** book?
- No, that's **his** book.
- That's **its** shelf.
- I'd like to see **their** bookshelves.

However, there are also **independent possessive pronouns.** These pronouns refer to a previously named or understood noun. They are: mine, ours, yours, his, hers, theirs.

- That's **mine**.
- Wrong. It's **ours**.
- Are these clothes **yours**?
- No, it's **theirs**

Independent possessive pronouns are stand alone and aren't followed by any other noun.

C Fill in each blank with the correct word from the brackets.

1. The net belongs to the fisherman. It is __________ (he, his, him).
2. The rabbits ran into a burrow. Is that burrow __________ (them, their, theirs, they)?

3. Grandmother is ill. These pills are __________ (she, her, hers).

4. The secret hideout is __________ (ours, our, us). Pam and I go there often.

5. Whose shirts are these? Are they __________ (you, yours, your)?

6. That boy is holding a stick. It is __________ (me, mine, my).

7. This is Mike's drink. This drink is __________ (he, him, his).

8. This is Sue and Tom's pet. This pet is __________ (they, theirs, their).

Relative Pronouns

Relative pronouns *refer to nouns mentioned previously. They are: who, whom, which, whoever, whomever, whichever, that.*

Examples:

- The driver **who** ran the stop sign was careless.
- The chair **which** you are sitting on is his.
- Take **whichever** ones you want.
- The car **that** crashed into the wall was silver.

D Fill in the blanks with the correct relative pronoun.

1. Here is someone __________ you simply must meet.

2. The cyclist __________ won the race had really trained hard.

3. He can choose one person, __________ he likes, to be his partner for that project.

4. This is the place __________ we met five years ago.

5. The trousers __________ you bought yesterday are already stained.

6. The baby, __________ nap had been interrupted, wailed loudly.

7. This is the drawer in __________ all the keys are kept.

8. This is the dog __________ was hit by a car last night?

9. The book, __________ it is finished, will be liked and appreciated.

10. I want to visit the place __________ my grandmother was born.

Demonstrative Pronouns

Demonstrative pronouns ***are used to point to something specific within a sentence. They can be singular or plural such as this, that, these, those.***

Examples:

- **These** are ugly.
- **Those** are lovely.
- Don't drink **this.**
- Did you see **that?**

E Underline the demonstrative pronouns.

1. These are nice shoes, but they look uncomfortable.
2. We saw that as we came in.
3. Are those your shoes?

4. Is this book yours?

5. Do you like these?

6. Look at that!

7. These are bigger than those.

8. This is heavier than that.

Interrogative Pronouns

Interrogative pronouns *are used to ask questions. An interrogative pronoun often appears at the beginning of a question. They are who, whom, which, what, whoever, whomever, whichever, whatever.*

Interrogative pronouns **who, whose** and **whom** are used to ask questions about people.

Examples:

- **Who** is going to the event?
- **Whose** car is this?
- **Whom** did you hand it over?

Interrogative pronouns **what** and **which** are used to ask questions about living and non-living things. Sometimes **which** is used to ask about people.

Examples:

- **What** are you bringing to the party?
- **Which** of these do you like better?
- **Which** one of the children is the winner?

F Fill in the blanks with the correct interrogative pronouns from the box. Some words can be used more than once.

whose	which	who	what	whom

1. __________ won the match yesterday?
2. __________ car was parked there just now?
3. __________ is the colour of her eyes?
4. __________ is the biggest building in the area?
5. __________ is at the door?
6. __________ did you visit yesterday?
7. __________ can we do here?
8. __________ books are these?

Reflexive Pronouns

Reflexive pronouns ***are used to show that the subject and the object of a sentence refer to the same person or thing. These pronouns end in -self or -selves. They are myself, yourself, , himself, herself, itself, ourselves, yourselves, themselves.***

Examples:

- I told **myself** not to spend all my money on new shoes.
- Richard stared at **himself** in the mirror.
- We gave **ourselves** plenty of extra time.
- They bought **themselves** a new car.

G Fill in the blanks with a suitable reflexive pronoun.

1. The actress had to put on her make-up ___________ before the show started.
2. "Wash the dishes ___________ after dinner", Mrs. Green told her two sons.
3. The kitten climbed the tree ___________.
4. "Trust only ___________. Do not trust anyone else", Sam told his brother.
5. My father repairs the electrical appliances at home ___________.
6. I have never made the bed ___________ before.
7. Annie only had ___________ to blame for this.
8. We did the work ___________.
9. My parents gave ___________ a holiday in Britain.
10. Annie told ___________ she should not be afraid of the dark.

ADJECTIVES

***An** adjective is a **describing word**. It is used to **describe people, place** or **things**.*

Possessive adjectives are the words that are used to *modify a noun* by showing *a form of possession or a sense of belonging* to a particular person or thing.

They are: **my, your, his, her, its, our and their.**

Examples:

- This is **my** book.
- Is that **your** book?
- I think it belongs to Sam. It must be **his** book.
- It belongs to Mary. It is **her** book.
- This is **our** house. **Their** house is down the street.

A Tick the correct word in the brackets in each sentence.

1. Mr. Anderson wants to cut (her, his) son's hair.
2. Nadia has handed (her, his) homework to the teacher.
3. My hands are clean. I washed (their, them) just now.
4. Where are Anthony's shoes? He seems to have lost (them, him).
5. We are supposed to leave (our, their) bags in the classroom during the break.
6. Look at the rhinoceros. (Its, his) skin is rough.
7. I write (our, my) secrets in this diary.
8. The students are writing (their, its) exams.

B Rewrite the sentences using possessive adjectives, without changing their meanings.

1. That cat is his.

 ____

2. The dinosaur is not yours.

 ____

3. This new house is theirs.

 ____

4. That doll is hers.

 ____

5. That prize is ours.

 ____

6. This coin is mine.

 ____

Other ways of showing possession

An **apostrophe** is normally **used** with the letter **'s'** to **show ownership** or **possession**. With most singular nouns, simply add an **apostrophe** plus the letter **'s'** to **do** this.

Example:

- This car belongs to Gary.
  This is Gary'**s** car.
- This umbrella belongs to Sophia.
  This is Sophia'**s** umbrella.

To make a **plural** noun **possessive**, simply add an **apostrophe** to the word. If the plural does not end in an **s,** then add an apostrophe plus **s.**

Examples:

- The girls' ribbons
  (The ribbons belonging to the girls.)
- The Wilsons' house
  (The Wilsons live in the house.)
- The men'**s** room
  (Plural does not end in **s.**)

C Use ('s) Or (') with the words in the brackets to show possession.

1. The __________ (pupils) belongings in the classroom were all stolen.
2. The __________ (women) husbands were unhappy with their cooking.
3. The __________ (ladies) hats are big and colourful.
4. The __________ (king) men went off on their horses to look for the prince's (prince) bride.
5. The robber snatched the __________ (policeman) gun.
6. The __________ (robber) fingerprints were all over the gun.
7. The officer took away the __________(workers) passports.
8. That dishonest boy borrowed this __________ (child) pen but did not return it.
9. The fire burnt down the __________ (people) homes.
10. There is a tattoo on the __________ (girl) arm.

D Rewrite each of the following sentences using the possessive form of the noun that is in bold.

1. Dolphins got caught in the nets that belong to the **fishermen.**

____

2. The seats in **Convention Hall** are comfortable

____

3. The teacher kept the windows of the **classroom** closed.

____

4. We brought a picnic basket of goodies made by **Mrs. Finch.**

____

5. The wife of my **boss** has invited me at her home.

____

6. The car that belonged to **John** is parked round the corner of the building.

____

7. The handles of **umbrellas** are sometimes carved.

____

8. The legs of the **tables** were all wobbly and needed repair.

____

COMPARISON OF ADJECTIVES

Comparative degree of adjectives ***are used to compare two nouns.***

Examples:

larger, smaller, faster, higher etc.

Superlative degree of adjectives ***are used to compare three or more nouns.***

Examples:

largest, smallest, fastest, highest etc.

Comparative adjectives

Comparative adjectives ***compare one person or thing with another and enable us to say whether a person or thing has more or less of a particular quality:***

Bobby is **taller than** his sister.

I'm **more interested** in music **than** sports.

We use the comparative with the word **than.**

Superlative adjectives

Superlative adjectives describe one person or thing as having more of a quality than all other people or things in a group:

Andrew is **the tallest** boy in the class.

This is **the most** precious gift I have ever received.

We use the superlative with the word **the.**

Spelling rules

One-syllable words that end in a double consonant (or two vowels and a single consonant) simply take the **-er** or **-est** at the end.

Examples:

Comparative	Superlative
Longer	Longest
Darker	Darkest
Brighter	Brightest
Quicker	Quickest
Warmer	Warmest
Colder	Coldest
Older	Oldest

When the adjective is only one syllable long and ends in a single vowel and a single consonant, we must double the final consonant, then add **-er** or **-est**.

Examples:

Comparative	Superlative
Bigger	Biggest
Fatter	Fattest
Hotter	Hottest
Sadder	Saddest
Thinner	Thinnest

- For the adjectives that end with a **y**, we replace the **y** with an **i**, then add **-er** or **-est** to form the comparative or the superlative.

Examples:

Comparative	Superlative
Prettier	Prettiest
Angrier	Angriest
Happier	Happiest
Thirstier	Thirstiest
Uglier	Ugliest

- For the adjectives that end with **e**, we must only add **-r** to make a comparative and **-st** to make a superlative.

Examples:

Comparative	Superlative
Wiser	Wisest
Stranger	Strangest
Looser	Loosest
Safer	Safest
Gentler	Gentlest
Simpler	Simplest

- If an adjective has three or more syllables add the word "more/less" before it to become comparative, and "most/ least" before it to become superlative.

Examples:

Comparative	Superlative
more beautiful	most beautiful
more interesting	most interesting
more delicious	most delicious
more important	most important
more enjoyable	most enjoyable

Irregular comparatives and superlatives

Some adjectives have **irregular forms** and we do not form the comparative and superlative degrees by adding **-er** or **-est** to the adjective.

Examples:

Adjective	Comparative	Superlative
good	better	best
bad	worse	worst
many	more	most
little	less	least
far	farther/further	farthest/furthest

Use of Comparative Adjective in a sentence

Here is a list of sentences making comparisons between two things:

- My house is **bigger** than yours.
- Your grade is **worse** than mine.
- My brother is **taller** than I am, but he is **older** too.
- The Earth is **larger** than the moon.

Use of Superlative Adjective in a sentence

Here are some examples of superlative adjectives in action:

- I can't find my **most comfortable** jeans.
- She is the **smartest** girl in our class.
- This is the **most interesting** book I have ever read.
- Mount Everest is the **highest** mountain in the world.

A Complete the table below.

Positive	Comparative	Superlative
	fairer	
lazy		
		most enjoyable
much		
	healthier	

B Underline the correct adjective in the brackets in each sentence.

1. This is the (big, bigger, biggest) compliment I have ever received.
2. I like this story. It is (interesting, more interesting, most interesting) than that story.
3. June is the (hot, hotter, hottest) month of the year.
4. This problem is (difficult, more difficult, most difficult) than the earlier one.
5. This laptop is the (expensive, more expensive, most expensive) one here.
6. Muthu's hair is (curly, curlier, curliest) than the girls'.
7. I will buy a (new, newer , newest) dress for the party.
8. The (quiet, quieter, quietest) my brother is, the more likely he is up to mischief.
9. This is the (tall, taller, tallest) building in the city.
10. My old house is (small, smaller, smallest) than my new one.

C Fill in the blanks with the correct form of the adjectives in the brackets.

1. The white shirt is the ____________ (clean).
2. I am feeling ____________(cold).
3. Yesterday was the ____________ (cold) day of the month so far.
4. Saba is the ____________ (pretty) of the two sisters.
5. Today's wind is ____________ (strong) than yesterday's.
6. Jane is the ____________ (quiet) girl in the family.
7. My house is ____________ (near) the market.

8. This river is the ____________ (wide) that I have seen.

9. Mr. Chang is ____________ (old) than Mr. Li.

10. Of all the tests, this one is the ____________ (easy).

11. This durian is not as ____________ (good) as that one.

12. This room is as ____________ (warm) as that room.

13. You must be more ____________ (careful) next time.

14. Today's lesson is more ____________ (boring) than yesterday's.

D Fill in the blanks with the correct form of the irregular adjectives in the brackets.

1. Ali has got __________ (good) results than Wasim.

2. Peter has got the __________ (good) results.

3. He has a __________ (bad) cut on his leg.

4. Yesterday was the __________ (bad) day of my life.

5. Tom has __________ (many) stamps than Brett.

6. There is __________ (much) water in the flask.

7. Carl is the __________ (good) student in the class.

8. This is a __________ (good) watch, sir.

9. We paid __________ (much) for this fish than for that fish.

10. We had a quiz. Ronny got the __________ (more) points. Tim got the __________ (little) points.

E **The table below compares five children in age, height, and weight. Fill in each blank using the correct form of the adjective in brackets.**

	Paul	Sue	Peter	John	Lisa
	9 years old	8 years old	10 years old	7 years old	6 years old
Height	137 cm	130 cm	135 cm	130 cm	128 cm
Weight	32 kg	28 kg	35 kg	30 kg	26 kg

1. Peter is the __________ (old) of all the children.
2. Lisa is the __________ (young) of all the children.
3. Paul is the __________ (tall) of all the children.
4. John is not as __________ (old) as Sue.
5. Lisa is __________ (short) than John and Sue.
6. Peter is the __________(heavy) in the group.
7. John is __________ (tall) than Lisa.

8. Sue is __________ (light) than john.

9. Sue is __________ (old) than Lisa, but __________ (young) than Peter.

10. John is __________ (light) than Peter, but __________ (heavy) than Sue.

F Rewrite the sentences given below using different degrees of comparison.

1. Shakespeare is the most famous of all writers in English.

____

____

2. Alia is the smartest girl in the class.

____

____

3. Iron is more useful than any other metal.

____

____

4. My father earns as much money as Mr. Bennet.

____

____

5. China is larger than India.

6. Greenland is the largest island in the world.

7. Air is lighter than water.

8. Very few metals are as costly as gold.

9. Mark is the strongest boy in the class.

10. He is better than any other player in the team.

VERB AND TENSE

Verb and tense

A time factor determines a verb's meaning as it indicates action or a state. This is called **tense**.

A present, past, or future action is recorded, respectively, in the present, past, or future time according to the rules of tense.

Example:

He **walks** to school. **(present tense)**

He **walked** to school. **(past tense)**

He **will walk** to school. **(future tense)**

Verbs in simple present tense

Verbs are used in the **simple present tense** when we talk about **facts, habits or something we know about a person or a thing.**

Examples:

- The sun rises in the east. **(fact)**
- He wakes up at 6 a.m. daily. **(habit)**
- The match starts at 9 o'clock. **(knowledge)**

Add **-s** or **-es** to a verb when used with **he, she, it** or a singular **noun**. Use a **plural verb (don't add -s or -es)** with **I, you, they, we** or a **plural noun**.

A **Fill in the blanks with the verb from the box in the simple present tense. Use each word only once.**

go	call	leave	play	sleep	bark	fly	get	expand	wash

1. Rachel __________ the home at 6. 30 a.m. for her morning walk.
2. Dogs __________ at strangers to scare them away.
3. Some birds __________ south for the winter.
4. Mrs. Waugh __________ to work by car every day.
5. Mother __________ up early in the morning to prepare breakfast for us.
6. Our cat __________ under our bed.
7. Metals __________ on heating.
8. George __________ his car once a week.
9. My mother __________ me daily.
10. We __________ in the neighbourhood park in the evening.

B **Fill in the blanks with the verb from the box in the simple present tense. Use each word only once.**

go	show	scan	keep	take
need	want	choose	contain	prints

The public libraries in Singapore are among the best in the world. They have many kinds of books that __________ information about real and imaginary people, places and events around the world.

If you ________ to the National Library, you may borrow up to four books at a time. You __________ a library card to do so. First you have to __________ the books that you __________ to borrow. Then you__________ them to the borrowing station. You __________ the books at a machine which __________ a receipt. It is important that you __________ all the receipts because they __________ the titles of the books you have borrowed and the date you __________ to return them.

Verbs in simple past tense

Verbs in the **simple past tense** are used to describe actions that happened in the **past**.

Regular and Irregular Verbs

A regular verb forms its **simple past tense** and its **past participle** by adding **-d, -ed** or **-ied** to the base form of the verb.

Regular Verb	Simple Past Tense	Past Participle
Sieve	Sieved	has sieved **(-d)**
Push	Pushed	has pushed **(-ed)**
Carry	Carried	has carried **(-ied)**

The past and past participle forms of irregular verbs either do not change or change in several ways.

Examples: No change

Irregular Verb	Simple Past Tense	Past Participle
Cut	Cut	has cut
Spread	Spread	has spread

Examples: change

Irregular Verb	Simple Past Tense	Past Participle
Tell	Told	has told
Bleed	Bled	has bled

C Fill in each blank with the simple past tense of the regular verb given in the brackets.

1. A baby kangaroo ____________ (hop) on to the road.
2. The milk ____________ (turn) sour when it went bad.
3. Penny ____________ (injure) herself yesterday while skiing.
4. The dentist ____________ (scale) my teeth last Monday.
5. My father ____________ (stop) fetching me from school when he ____________ (start) his new job a few months ago.
6. She ____________ (complain) of an acute headache last night.
7. The salesman at the store ____________ (accuse) the fat guy with a beard of stealing.
8. The teacher ____________ (scold) Amber for coming late to the class.
9. Agnes ____________ (walk) into the room with a big smile.
10. The policemen ____________ (chase) the thief and caught him.

D Fill in each blank with the simple past tense of the irregular verb given in the brackets.

1. Jessica ____________ (carry) her luggage to the car herself.
2. Peter ____________ (drive) around for two hours to look for parking.
3. Marsh____________ (forget) to give my mother's message.

4. I accidentally __________ (get) chewing gum in my hair.

5. India __________ (beat) West Indies in the 1983 World Cup final to become first time champions.

6. We __________ (go) to California last year.

7. The dog jumped out of the swimming pool and __________ (shake) himself.

8. The vase __________ (fall) off the table and ________ (break) into pieces.

9. He __________ (bend) the branch until it __________ (break).

10. He __________(leap) into the air with joy when he __________ (learn) that he was __________ (choose) the captain of the team.

E Rewrite the following sentences in the simple past tense.

1. Sam wins a prize in the competition.

____

2. Penny lose all her sheep and weeps.

____

3. The show ends and everyone goes home feeling good.

____

4. The robber hides behind the door.

____

5. The teacher tells her to go home.

____

6. Mrs. Bennett teaches us Science.

____

F Fill in each blank with the simple present or simple past tense of the word given in the brackets.

1. The nurse ____________ (wheel) the patient from the intensive care unit to the ward.
2. Penny ____________ (make) Christmas greeting cards every year.
3. Maggie and I ____________ (play) together every day.
4. The workers ____________ (finish) their work at 6 p.m. and left.
5. This bicycle ____________ (belong) to Mathew but he seldom ____________ (ride) them.
6. Brenda ____________ (cook) her own lunch every afternoon.
7. Many passersby ____________ (stop) to help the accident victim.
8. He ____________ (make) him ____________ (pay) for the damage to his car.
9. This store ____________ (open) at 10 a.m. every day.
10. The hotel guests ____________ (panic) and ____________ (scream) at the sound of the guns.

Present Continuous Tense and Past Continuous Tense

Present Continuous Tense talks about an action which is **still going on now or going to be continued in future**. It uses **am/is/are** and **-ing** is added with the verb.

Example

- It **is raining** cats and dogs. (It is still raining heavily.)
- They **are going** to Sentosa tomorrow. (continued in future)

Past Continuous Tense talks about an action which was **in progress at some time in the past.**

Example

- It **was raining** heavily this morning.
- Amber **was waiting** for Marsha at home all day when she sent her the message.

We use the **past continuous tense** form of a verb to mark an **action that was going on when a second one took place.**

Example

- She **was playing** the piano while there was a loud knock at the door.
- We **were cycling** when the accident happened.

G Fill in the blanks with the present continuous tense form of the verbs in the brackets.

1. A man ____________ (wait) at the door.
2. Many people ____________ (switch) to trains.
3. Car drivers ____________ (get) angry because they cannot find parking space.
4. I ____________ (sing) at the auditorium today.
5. I ____________ (meet) my friends after school.
6. ______ you ____________ (visit) the doctor in the evening today?
7. We ____________ (go) for a movie this weekend.
8. The telephone ____________ (ring).
9. The policemen on the bike ____________ (chase) the car thief.
10. He ____________ (study) to become a doctor.

H Change the given verbs in brackets into present continuous tense forms to complete the description in the following paragraph.

Mrs. Shaun ____________ (shop) for groceries. She ____________ (wonder) what to cook as a lot of guests ____________ (come) in the evening for dinner. Mr. and Mrs. Shaun ____________ (celebrate) their daughter Sara's sixteenth birthday. Mrs. Shaun ____________ (plan) to cook something unique.

Brett, Sara's brother ____________ (decorate) the hall all by himself. He is helping (help) his parents. They all ____________ (plan) to give Sara a surprise.

I Fill in the blanks with the past continuous tense form of the verbs in the brackets.

1. While we ________________ the movie in the cinema hall, the rain began.
2. I ________________ a scary dream when the alarm clock rang.
3. Alex ________________ the grass the other day when the snake appeared.

4. Abbey ________________ to New Zealand for his new job but changed his mind later.

5. I ________________ not ________________ when you got home late last night.

6. I ________________ for my audition when he interrupted me.

7. I ________________ to my music, so I didn't hear the phone ring.

8. The toddler ________________ when the lion took him away.

9. While she ________________ to her friend, someone snatched her phone.

10. I ________________ dinner when the doorbell rang.

11. I ________________ if you could walk the dog for me this evening.

12. We ________________ up the mountains when it started to rain.

J Fill in the blanks with the correct past continuous tense or simple past tense form of the verbs in the brackets.

1. I ______________ (do) my science project when he __________ (knock) at the door.

2. I ______________ (walk) to the shopping mall alone when I __________ (meet) an old friend.

3. The men ______________ (fish) along the river when the earthquake ______________ (strike).

4. I ______________ (wait) for the bus when I __________ (see) her.

5. I was ______________ (sleep) when he ___________ (come).

6. Mr. Li was ______________(read) a magazine when the phone __________ (ring).

7. The monkeys were ______________ (sit) in a tree when the naughty boys ___________ (start) throwing stones at them.

8. Alan was ______________ (wash) his father's car when it ____________ (start) to rain.

9. A customer ______________ (come) in just as he was____________ (open) his lunch box.

10. Betty __________ (find) a gent's wallet on the road as she was ____________ (walk) home one day.

11. Power supply __________ (go) off when we were ______________ (have) dinner.

12. My mother was ______________ (cook) dinner when I ______________ (reach) home.

The Future Tense

Future tense talks about an action that has **not yet happened** or a **state that does not yet exist.**

Future tense is formed by

a. using **shall** or **will** with a verb in its base form. **(Simple Future Tense)**

- **Shall** or **will** are used with **I**.
- **Will** is used with **you, he, she, it, we** and **they**.
- Using **'going to'** with the verb.

Example

- I **will** go to my friend's birthday.
- Ken is **going to take** photographs tomorrow.

b. using **will be** with **present participle. (Future Continuous Tense)**

Example

- I **will be playing** for an hour.

c. using **will have** with **the past participle of the main verb**. **(Future Perfect Tense)**

Example

- She **will have arrived** by lunch.

d. using **will have been** with the **base form of the verb + -ing**. **(Future Perfect Continuous Tense)**

Example:

- I **will have been walking** for 3 hours.

K Fill in the blanks with the simple future tense forms of the verbs in the brackets.

1. I ______________ (drive) to Montreal this weekend.
2. We ______________ (move) to Texas next month.
3. It ______________ (rain) tomorrow.
4. I ______________ (study) hard for exams.

5. I ______________ (prepare) dinner today.

6. I ______________ (learn) a new language.

7. It ______________ (rain) tomorrow.

8. Betty ______________ (read) that book.

9. Mother ______________ (prefer) coffee to tea.

10. We ______________ (enjoy) the musical drama.

11. You ______________ (meet) a beautiful girl.

12. I ______________ (attend) a program at my varsity on Friday.

L Fill in the blanks with the future continuous tense forms of the verbs in the brackets.

1. I ____________________ (write) articles on different topics.

2. The baby ____________________ (walk) soon.

3. They ____________________ (play) at this time tomorrow.

4. We ____________________ (sail) in an hour.

5. I ____________________ (not, attend) the program because of my busy schedule.

6. The train ____________________ (leave) in half an hour.

7. They ____________________ (play) football in that field.

8. He ____________________ (not, study) all afternoon.

9. He ________________ (attend) the seminar today.

10. This time next Monday we ________________ (leave) for California.

11. We ________________ (watch) a movie in this Cineplex on next Friday.

12. He ________________ (sing) different kinds of songs on the stage.

13. George ________________ (travel) around the world in March.

14. He ________________ (learn) how to drive a car next week.

15. They ________________ (play) semi final tomorrow.

16. At 7 a.m. tomorrow she ________________ (exercise) in the gym.

17. The poet ________________ (write) a romantic poem for the program.

18. This time tomorrow I ________________ (lie) on the beach.

19. ________________ (you, go) to the concert of realistic songs?

20. Within a month, I ________________ (swim) like a pro.

M Fill in the blanks with the future perfect tense forms of the verbs in the brackets.

1. She ________________ (finish) the job by the end of this month.

2. I ________________ (complete) the assignment by Monday.

3. The children ________________ (reach) home by the time their father returns from work.

4. She ________________ (clean) the house before her father comes.

5. By the time you get this letter, I ____________________(leave).

6. Alex ____________________ (submit) the tender by tomorrow.

7. The fire ____________________ (destroy) the whole building before the firemen arrive.

8. She ____________________ (leave) before you reach her house.

9. They ____________________ (finish) making the bridge by January.

10. The patient ____________________ (die) before they reach the hospital.

11. Peter ____________________ (go) to the library before he comes to the class.

12. We ____________________ (shop) in that market before you come home.

13. The children ____________________ (eat) all the cake before their mother comes.

14. You ____________________ (read) the lesson before the next class.

15. I ____________________ (attend) the program before I come here.

16. They ____________________ (arrive) by dinner time.

17. ____________________ (they, finish) assignment by seven?

18. She ____________________ (clean) the house by the time she leaves the house.

19. He ____________________ (teach) us for 6 months by next week.

20. She ____________________ (return) from the school by 3 o'clock.

N Fill in the blanks with the future perfect continuous tense forms of the verbs in the brackets.

1. They ______________________ (wait) for the chief guest for 2 hours.
2. Francis ______________________ (stay) at his grandma's place for three weeks.
3. By the end of the month I ______________________ (live) in this town for ten years.
4. Samantha ______________________ (work) at the summer camp for six weeks.
5. Kevin ______________________ (study) in the library for 3 hours.
6. We ______________________ (shop) in that market before you come home.
7. Naomi ______________________ (attend) driving school for quite a long time.
8. I ______________________ (learn) French for a year by the time I leave for France.
9. Will ______________________ (they, travel) for long when they arrive?
10. Roger ______________________ (teach) for five years by the time he's 30.
11. Suzie ______________________ (live) here for a year next month.
12. She ______________________ (sleep) for three hours by noon.

ADVERBS

An **adverb** is a word that **describes a verb, an adjective, another adverb, a phrase, a clause, or a sentence.**

An **adverbial phrase** is an adverb that has **more than one word**. It usually starts with a preposition.

Example:

- The cat purrs **happily.**
- The cat purrs in a **contended way.**

Both the adverb **happily** and the adverbial phrase **in a contended way** describe the verb **purr.**

Types of adverbs

Adverbs of Manner

An **adverb of manner** tells us how an action is carried out.

Example:

- She passed the exam **easily.**
- The lion roars **loudly.**

Very often, adverbs of manner are formed by adding **-ly or -ily** (in the words that end in **-y**) to the end of an adjective.

Example:

loud**ly**, slow**ly**, quick**ly**, heavi**ly**, etc.

Some adverbs of manner take the same spelling as the adjective and do not add an -ly to the end:

Example:

- The boys had worked **hard**.
- Julia dances **well**.

A Fill in the blanks with the correct adverbs from the box.

strongly	hurriedly	bitterly	noisily	greedily	painfully
anxiously	heavily	quickly	loudly	carefully	eagerly

1. She wept ____________ when she heard the news.

2. The policeman knocked ____________ on the door.

3. Walk ____________ or you may miss the bus.

4. Sara fell ____________ down the steps.

5. She waited ____________ for her mother to arrive to give her the good news.

6. He ate all the pastries ____________.

7. He got dressed ____________ as he was getting late for his exam.

8. She glanced around the room ____________.

9. The wind blew ____________ from the south.

10. Choose your words ____________ when you speak.

11. The pile of books fell ____________ on the floor.

12. The patient walked ____________ on crutches.

PREPOSITION

A **preposition** is a **word** or a **set of words** that are used to link a **person, place, animal or thing to other words within the sentence.**

It tells us if the words are related by **place, direction, time, or manner.**

Example:

- He sat **on** the chair. (place)
- She swam **across** the lake. (direction)
- Let's meet **before** noon. (time)
- He goes to work **by** train. (manner)

Types of prepositions

1. **Preposition of place (spatial)**
   These prepositions are used to illustrate the location of nouns or **pronouns** in a sentence.

   Example: In, On, Between, Behind, Under, Over, Near, etc.

2. **Preposition for direction** These are used to describe the movement of one noun or pronoun towards another noun or pronoun.

   Example: to, into, towards, through, etc.

3. **Preposition of time** These are used when there is a need to indicate when a particular event happened.

   Example: In, On, At, Since, For, During, etc.

4. **Preposition for manner** These are applied to describe the way or means by which something happened or happens, when used in a sentence.

   Example: On, In, With, By, Like, etc.

A Tick the correct preposition in the sentences below.

1. Peter is in front of / next to Mary.
2. Annie is among / beside Mary.
3. Mary is above / between Peter and Annie.

4. The child is sitting on / under the stool.
5. The stool is on / under the woman.
6. The lady is behind / near the child.

B Choose the appropriate preposition of place from the words in brackets and fill in the blanks.

1. Jessie waited for Jim _______ the corner. (in/ on/ at)
2. The worried mother sat ___________ her sick child all night. (above, beside, near)
3. The engine is _________ the car's bonnet. (above/ across/ under)
4. We spent a quiet evening _______ home. (at/ in/ on)
5. London is _______ the river Thames. (in/ on/ at)
6. The cat was hiding __________ the door. (under/ above/ behind)
7. The chief guest is sitting ____________ the president and the prime minister. (near/ beside/ between)
8. An unidentified plane had travelled __________ the Malay peninsula. (near/ across/ in)
9. What's _______ the menu this evening? (on/ in/ at)
10. I like the painting hanging _______ the wall. (in/ over/ on)

C Fill in the blanks with an appropriate preposition of direction from the words in the clue box. Use each preposition only once.

around	onto	out	next to	into	across	up to	up
through	towards	past	from	out of	by	in	

1. She was carrying a suitcase and walking _____________ him.
2. They drove ____________ the tunnel.

3. He walked away __________ me.

4. They told stories __________ the campfire.

5. The thrift store is ________ the church.

6. The library is __________ the post office.

7. My friend lives __________ the street from me.

8. The dog climbed __________ the bed.

9. She drove right __________ the house.

10. As Samantha was climbing __________ the swimming pool, she slipped and fell back __________.

11. Although we can take an elevator __________ the top of the building, we decided to walk __________ the staircase.

12. She didn't have any difficulty pulling __________ the parking space, but as she was backing __________, she scratched the car next to her.

D Fill in the blanks with an appropriate preposition of time.

1. Sophie was born _______ October 28, 2000.

2. We waited _______ half past six for you.

3. Birds often migrate _______ spring and autumn.

4. He is staying in London _______ the June 30th.

5. The bank is open _______ 8:00 a.m. _______ 5:00 p.m. Monday through Saturday.

6. I have an appointment with the doctor _______ 5:00 p.m.

7. My great-grandmother is always up _______ dawn.

8. She quit her job in January and started her own company two months _______.

9. I am just going to bed _______ an hour or so.

10. I felt fairly relaxed _______ taking the medicine.

11. He had promised to be back _______ 5 o'clock.

12. I've been waiting _______ ten o'clock.

E Fill in the blanks with the correct prepositions from the brackets.

1. I took my hat ________ (of, off) the table.

2. We walked ________ (despite, past) the restaurant.

3. The store is open daily ________ (for, from) Monday to Saturday.

4. The treasure was hidden ________ (under, up to)the earth.

5. The children ran ________ (of, out of) the school.

6. The bank is ________ (opposite, below) the hospital.

7. Nocturnal animals usually sleep ________ (during, underneath) the day.

8. I will work ________ (until, by) six o' clock.

9. 'A' comes ________ (before, behind) 'B' in the alphabet.

10. He opened the box ________ (by, with) a screwdriver.

CONJUNCTIONS

A **conjunction** is a **joining word.** It connects **words or groups of words.**

Conjunctions are also called **connectors.** Some **connectors** are : **and, or, but, as well as, both, not only... but also etc.**

Example:

- She likes music **and** singing dance.
- She likes music **as well as** dance.
- She likes **both** music **and** dance.
- She not only likes music **but also** likes dance.

Types of conjunctions

There are **three basic types of conjunctions:**

1. **coordinating conjunctions**
2. **subordinating conjunctions**
3. **correlative conjunctions.**

Coordinating conjunctions

It shows that the **parts of the sentence that it connects are of equal importance.** Some coordinating conjunctions include **and, but, or, not, for, so , yet, because, etc.**

Example:

- Jeremy is tall **and** thin.
- The treasure was hidden in the cave **or** in the underground lagoon.
- Alison is clever **but** lazy.
- We didn't like the show, **so** we left.

Subordinating conjunctions

It shows that **one part of a sentence is dependent on another.** The part that is dependent is introduced by conjunctions such as **when, while, where, whereas, since, so that, as, than, if, even, though, before, after, etc.**

Example:

- We left early **because** it was already late.
- **When** you are called, you must come in at once.
- You will get a promotion **if** you deserve it.
- I arrived **after** they had gone.

Correlative conjunctions

Correlative conjunctions also connect sentences of equal importance, but **they work in pairs.** They include pairs such as **either...or, neither...nor, not only...but also, both.... also, such... that, etc.**

Example:

- She is **so** smart **that** she answered all the questions.
- I want **neither** vanilla ice cream **nor** strawberry ice cream.
- **Either** you **or** I am wrong.
- There was **such** great pain **that** he could not stop his tears.

A **Fill in the blanks with the correct words from the box. Use each word only once. There may be more than one possible answer.**

and	but	or	because	so

Conner fell ill ________ he could not wash ________ feed the elephants. The other zoo keepers wanted to help him ________ they can only do so at two o' clock ____________ they had to finish their own work first. They had to feed the elephants sugarcane ________ leaves.

B Underline the conjunctions in the following sentences and state whether they are coordinating, subordinating, or correlative.

1. She was ill, but she went to work.

    ____

2. She'd rather play the drums than sing.

    ____

3. We arrived after they left.

    ____

4. Although he was strong, he could not defeat his opponent.

    ____

5. Plastic is not only cheap but also a durable product.

    ____

6. You will not get the prize unless you deserve it.

    ____

7. Because the night was young, Gertrude decided to take a walk.

    ____

8. I go to the park every Sunday, for I long to see his face.

    ____

9. Since you have apologised, we will not take any further action against you.

    ____

ANSWER KEY

Noun

(A)

1. Common noun
2. Proper Noun
3. Proper Noun
4. Common noun, Common noun
5. Common noun
6. Proper Noun, Common Noun
7. Proper Noun, Proper Noun
8. Common noun , Common noun

(B)

Proper noun	Common Noun
1. Rita	market, vegetables
2. Ayush	kit, house
3.	brother, dentist
4.	aunt, lady
5. Mr. Stilton	writer
6. Akbar	emperor
7.	road

Collective Nouns

(A)

1. crowd
2. bouquet
3. choir
4. fleet
5. pack
6. library
7. shoal
8. swarm

(B)

lions	-	pride
ants	-	colony
cards	-	pack
birds	-	flock
soldiers	-	army
footballers	-	team
cows	-	herd
bread slices	-	loaf

Pronoun

(A)

Hello, my name is Peter. **I** live in the city with my mother and father and two sisters. My father is a teacher. **He** works very long hours. My mother is a lawyer, but **she** only works part - time. My sisters and I try to help our parents as much as **we** can. My sisters help in the kitchen. **They** wash and dry the dishes. **I** make my own bed and keep my room tidy. **We** have a cat called Ginger. **It** has lived with **us** for a long time.

(B)

1. Eiffel Tower
2. Dad and I
3. Andrew, Tom
4. Sonia
5. Wind
6. John, Sue, I
7. Computer
8. Shoes
9. Alice
10. Tim

(C)

1. his
2. theirs
3. hers
4. ours
5. yours
6. mine
7. his
8. theirs

(D)

1. whom
2. who
3. whomever
4. where
5. that
6. whose
7. which
8. that
9. when
10. where

(E)

1. These
2. that
3. those
4. this
5. these
6. that
7. These **and** those
8. This **and** that

(F)

1. Who
2. Whose
3. What
4. Which
5. Who
6. Whom
7. What
8. Whose

(G)

1. herself
2. yourselves
3. itself
4. yourself
5. himself
6. myself
7. herself
8. ourselves
9. themselves
10. herself

Adjectives

Possessive Adjectives

(A)

1. his
2. her
3. them
4. them
5. our
6. Its
7. my
8. their

(B)

1. That is his cat.
2. It is not your dinosaur.
3. This is their new house.
4. That is her doll.
5. That is our prize.
6. This is my coin.

(C)

1. pupils'
2. women's
3. ladies'
4. king's
5. policeman's
6. robber's
7. workers'
8. child's
9. people's
10. girl's

(D)

1. Dolphins got caught in the fishermen's nets.
2. The Convention Hall's seats are comfortable.
3. The teacher kept the classroom's door closed.
4. We brought a picnic basket of Mrs. Finch's goodies.
5. My boss's wife has invited me at her home.
6. John's car is parked round the corner of the building.
7. Umbrellas' handles are sometimes carved.
8. The tables' legs were all wobbly and needed repair.

Comparison of Adjectives

(A)

fair	fairer	fairest
lazy	lazier	laziest
enjoyable	more enjoyable	most enjoyable
much	more	most
healthy	healthier	healthiest

(B)

1. biggest
2. more interesting
3. hottest
4. more difficult
5. most expensive
6. curlier
7. new
8. quieter
9. tallest
10. smaller

(C)

1. cleanest
2. cold
3. coldest
4. prettier
5. stronger
6. quietest
7. near
8. widest
9. older
10. easiest
11. good
12. warm
13. careful
14. boring

(D)

1. better
2. best
3. bad
4. worst
5. more
6. more
7. best
8. good
9. more
10. most **and** least

(E)

1. oldest
2. youngest
3. tallest
4. old
5. shorter
6. heaviest
7. taller
8. lighter
9. older **and** younger
10. lighter **and** heavier

(F)

1. No other writer in English is as famous as Shakespeare. / Shakespeare is greater than any other writer in English.
2. No other girl in the class is as smart as Alia.
   Alia is smarter than any other girl in the class.
3. No other metal is as useful as iron. / Iron is the most useful of all metals.
4. Mr. Bennet does not earn more money than my father.
5. India is not as large as China.
6. Greenland is larger than any other island in the world. / No other island in the world is as large as Greenland.
7. Water is not as light as air.
8. Gold is costlier than most other metals.
9. Mark is stronger than any other boy in the class. / No other boy in the class is as strong as Mark.
10. He is the best player in the team.

Verb and Tense

(A)

1. leaves
2. bark
3. fly
4. goes
5. gets
6. sleeps
7. expand
8. washes
9. calls
10. play

(B)

The public libraries in Singapore are among the best in the world. They have many kinds of books that **contain** information about real and imaginary people, places and events around the world.
If you **go** to the National Library, you may borrow up to four books at a time. You **need** a library card to do so. First you have to **choose** the books that you **want** to borrow. Then you **take** them to the borrowing station. You **scan** the books at a machine which **prints** a receipt. It is important that you **keep** all the receipts because they **show** the titles of the books you have borrowed and the date you **have** to return them.

(C)

1. hopped
2. turned
3. injured
4. scaled
5. stopped **and** started
6. complained
7. accused
8. scolded
9. walked
10. chased

(D)

1. carried
2. drove
3. forgot
4. got
5. beat
6. went
7. shook
8. fell **and** broke
9. bent **and** broke
10. leaped, learnt **and** chosen

(E)

1. Sam won a prize in the competition.
2. Penny lost all her sheep and wept.
3. The show ended and everyone went home feeling good.
4. The robber hid behind the door.
5. The teacher told her to go home.
6. Mrs. Bennett taught us Science.

(F)

1. wheeled
2. makes
3. play
4. finished
5. belongs **and** rides
6. cooks
7. stopped
8. made and pay
9. opens
10. panicked and screamed

(G)

1. is waiting
2. are switching
3. are getting
4. am singing
5. am meeting
6. are and visiting
7. are going
8. is ringing
9. are chasing
10. is studying

(H)

Mrs. Shaun is **shopping** (shop) for groceries. She is **wondering** (wonder) what to cook as a lot of guests are **coming** (come) in the evening for dinner. Mr. and Mrs. Shaun are **celebrating** (celebrate) their daughter Sara's sixteenth birthday. Mrs. Shaun is **planning** (plan) to cook something unique.
Brett, Sara's brother is **decorating** (decorate) the hall all by himself. He is **helping** (help) his parents . They all are **planning** (plan) to give Sara a surprise.

(I)

1. were watching
2. was having
3. was cutting
4. was going
5. was **and** sleeping
6. was practicing
7. was listening
8. was crying
9. was talking
10. was cooking
11. was wondering
12. were climbing

(J)

1. was doing **and** knocked
2. was walking **and** met
3. were fishing **and** struck
4. was waiting **and** saw
5. was sleeping **and** came
6. was reading **and** rang
7. were sitting **and** started
8. was washing **and** started
9. came **and** was opening
10. found **and** walking
11. went **and** were having
12. was cooking **and** reached

(K)

1. will drive
2. will move
3. will rain
4. shall study
5. will prepare
6. will learn
7. will rain
8. will read
9. will prefer
10. will enjoy
11. will meet
12. will attend

(L)

1. will be writing
2. will be walking
3. will be playing
4. will be sailing
5. will not be attending
6. will be leaving
7. will be playing
8. will not be studying
9. will be attending
10. will be leaving
11. will be watching
12. will be singing
13. will be travelling
14. will be learning
15. will be playing
16. will be exercising
17. will be writing
18. I will be lying
19. Will you be going
20. will be swimming

(M)

1. will have finished
2. shall have completed
3. will have reached
4. will have cleaned
5. will have left
6. will have submitted
7. will have destroyed
8. will have left
9. will have finished
10. will have died
11. will have gone
12. will have shopped
13. will have eaten
14. will have read
15. will have attended
16. will have arrived
17. will they have finished
18. will have cleaned
19. will have taught
20. will have returned

(N)

1. will have been waiting
2. will have been staying
3. will have been living
4. will have been working
5. will have been studying
6. will have been shopping
7. will have been attending
8. will have been learning
9. Will they have been travelling
10. will have been teaching
11. will have been living
12. will have been sleeping

Adverbs

(A)

1. bitterly
2. loudly
3. quickly
4. heavily
5. eagerly
6. greedily
7. hurriedly
8. anxiously
9. strongly
10. carefully

11. noisily
12. painfully

Preposition

(A)

1. next
2. beside
3. between
4. on
5. under
6. near

(B)

1. at
2. beside
3. under
4. at
5. on
6. behind
7. between
8. across
9. on
10. on

(C)

1. towards
2. through
3. from
4. around
5. by
6. next to
7. across
8. onto
9. past
10. out of **and** in
11. up to **and** up
12. into **and** out

(D)

1. on
2. until
3. in
4. until
5. from and to
6. at
7. before
8. later
9. for
10. after
11. by
12. since

(E)

1. off
2. past
3. from
4. under
5. out of
6. opposite
7. during
8. until
9. before
10. with

Conjunctions

(A)

Conner fell ill **so** he could not wash **and** feed the elephants. The other zoo keepers wanted to help him **but** they can only do so at two o' clock **because** they had to finish their own work first. They had to feed the elephants sugarcane **or** leaves.

(B)

1. but - coordinating conjunction
2. rather...than – correlative conjunction
3. after – subordinating conjunction
4. although – subordinating conjunction
5. not only... but also– correlative conjunction
6. unless – subordinating conjunction
7. because- subordinating conjunction
8. for – coordinating conjunction
9. since – subordinating conjunction

WORK SPACE

WORK SPACE